TAKEN for PEARLS

Also by Tony Curtis:

Poetry

Album

Preparations

Letting go

Selected Poems 1970-85

Poems Selected & New (USA)

The Last Candles

Anthologies

Pembrokeshire Poems

The Poetry of Snowdonia

The Poetry of Pembrokeshire

Love from Wales (with Siân James)

Criticism

Dannie Abse (Writers of Wales Series)

Wales: The Imagined Nation   ed.

The Art of Seamus Heaney   ed.

How to Study Modern Poetry

TAKEN for PEARLS

new poems
by
Tony Curtis

SEREN BOOKS

SEREN BOOKS
is the book imprint of
Poetry Wales Press Ltd.
Andmar House, Tondu Road
Bridgend, Mid-Glamorgan

© Tony Curtis, 1993

Cataloguing in Publication Data:
Curtis, Tony
Taken for Pearls
I. Title
821.914

ISBN:1-85411-087-X

The Publisher acknowledges the financial assistance of the
Welsh Arts Council

Printed and bound by
WBC, Bridgend, Mid Glam.

Cover Painting by Otto Dix 'Portrait of the Painter Hans Theo Richter
and his wife Gisela, Dresden, 1933' courtesy of Galerie Der Stadt,
Stuttgart, Germany.

Contents

7 Taken for Pearls
8 Pembrokeshire Buzzards
9 Judy
10 At the Border
12 Under the Yew
14 Playing for Vince
16 Angel on the Line
17 A Sloping House
19 Haiku
20 Rope Tricks
21 Aubade
22 Coracle
23 Reg Webb
24 Walking on Water
26 The New Settlement
28 Sutherland at Picton Ferry
30 *Two Augustus John Poems*
30   Caitlin Macnamara
32   Inspiration
33 The Captain's Diary
37 Playing St. Enodoc's
39 The Poetry of Money
41 *Translations:*
    Five Poems from the Dialect
    of the Iraqi Marsh Arabs
    by Mudhafer Al Nawab
43   To the Train and Hammad
46   Knocked Flat
47   A Liar
48   Twice Robbed
49   The Summer-rain is Coming

51   The Pew
52   More and more
53   The Eagle
54   Soap Opera
55   Coeurs de Plomb
56   Queen's Tears
58   Summer in Bangkok
60   In Union Square, 1978
62   Brady's Glass
63   From the hills, the town
64   Belgium: Coffee
65   Incident on a hospital train from Calcutta, 1944
66   The Night-trees
67   Portrait of the Painter Hans Theo Richter
       and his wife Gisela, Dresden, 1933
69   The Visit to Terezin
70   The bowl and the spoon
71   Acknowledgements
72   About the Author

Taken for Pearls

In muddied waters the eyes of fishes
are taken for pearls.

As those two trout, little bigger than my hand then,
taken by spinner at Cresselly on an early

summer's day in the quiet afternoon
before the season's traffic. Only

a tractor in an unseen field
stitching the air like a canopy over it all.

And the taste of them pan-fried nose to tail
by my mother. The sweet flesh prised from

cages of the most skilfully carved bone.
I closed my eyes and she smiled for me.

Pembrokeshire Buzzards

The buzzards of my boyhood days are back again,
their wide-stretched, ragged wings
like distant, emblematic kites. Our speed brings
them close to, still as icons, precisely drawn.

A single blown buzzard's egg nested in Pwllcrochan
at the centre of gull, wren and blackbird
in my shotgun-toting cousin's collection,
coffined in the shoe-box under his bed.

For twenty years since then, in my middle time,
they were rare. It seemed they had gone too
the way of the plagued rabbits. The oily spew
of the refineries, the tourists' fumes

and farmers' chemicals had seen them off. But
now the buzzards of my growing years are back.
Each road, every deep, high-hedged track
is reigned over by a pair — imperious, vigilant.

Where did they go? All these years.
Somewhere unseen, perched high in pylons, poles and trees
their clawed, bobbing weight was riding always.
Above our speeding car, memories lift off the wires.

Judy

got so bad she couldn't stand or eat,
just lay there on the carpet
loose-jawed and messing from both ends.

My father said it was thirteen
years next month and let her go on
until even my mother said it was enough.

Then he wrapped Judy up in an old blanket
and drove off.
He came back late and stinking but

we didn't say a thing.
He fell asleep in front of the tv.
and we left him there.

The last thing I remember that night —
my mother easing off his shoes
and sitting there on the settee,

his slippers in her hands, eyes
closed, holding them in her lap,
warm, smelling of dog.

At the Border

When I tilt the can over the herb border
she's planted, no water comes.
I tilt again, but still nothing shows.
Leaves, I suppose, have clogged
the spout from last autumn, rotted and plugged
so the water's locked in.

With both hands I lift to eye level
the laden, awkward can and tip again.
This roadside gift fallen from a builder's truck,
battered and cement-stained, with no rose,
has been ours for three different gardens. It won't work,
and I am miming in that silent film
where the children have stepped on the hose.

I lower it and shake, until from the sharp funnel
emerges like a pencil lead the beak
and then the head of a bird.
I make the water force it halfway through
until the shoulders clear and it thrusts
like some bow-sprit figure from the spout.
It is absurd and saddening — its eyes shut,
a blind, futile arrow.

One of this spring's young, curious,
has flown into the can's nesting dark
where I left it safe under the sycamores
and, soft thing, after its flutter
in the echoing space has chosen
that jewel of light promised at the spout
before the easy freedom of the can's wide brim.

Pointing its way up the shaft of blue sky
this days-old starling
wormed its way into a coffin of light
which tightened and starved it in the mildest of springs.
Now, in the early summer sun, I lift the can once more
and force the bird in a shower of wet light
out and into the herb border.

Safe from the magpies and neighbours' cats
in the musk of rosemary and marjoram,
worked by the weather, bone and feather
break down into soil that
feeds our parsley, chives and thyme.

Under the Yew

Gran, it's me. Passing through.
I've stopped again and bought these daffs for you.

No, it's the beginning of February.
They fly them in from somewhere now — Jersey,
abroad. They force them in greenhouses.
They're wiry and all the same
as if someone stamped them out on a machine,
but they'll last weeks
in the rain-water your urn's filled for them.
The cover had blown off with its dry sticks
of whatever they were I left last time
from the other side of Christmas. I've put it back.

I'm losing my feet, such terrible winds we have now.
That's all to do with greenhouses too,
but explaining would take more time than I've got,
Gran, and it's more than I really know.

The yew in front and to the left of you
is down like a drunk old man. The earth still
clings to its roots, out in the daylight
after god knows how many years. It fell
last week in the last gales, no doubt.
The one behind that overhangs your plot
has weathered firm enough. Shelter for years to come
and, I suppose, shade and shelter enough for my time.

There's blue sky, but not enough to patch a sleeve,
and the rain hammers down today like nails.
The Towy's up to the brim of the fields and about to spill.
At least driving home I'll go east before the weather.

It will be a month or two now, I expect
I come down to work, or just to see Mum.
Dad's so much dust on the coast path at Lydstep,
and that's nothing like the same.

I fly to America, Hong Kong, all over the place,
but the string is tied back here, as they say —
apron strings, heart strings, a way through the maze.

      The time. I have to go now.
The rain's coming hard again.
The motorway will be awash and dangerous as glass.
Everyone does such speed now, Gran.

Take care. And I'll take care.

Playing for Vince

The next morning I went over early.
The changing room floor still wet,
but everything in place as it should be.
I fed the meter and lit the scuffed, white court.

Then Bob came and we warmed up the ball,
driving it at the front wall between the lines
— forehand, backhand, change over,
spin rough or smooth for serve.

And we played. Stiffly at first,
going through the motions, then warming up
and believing in it, thumping against
the wall, the clattered tin.
Both knowing that this had to be done,
now, this morning, for Vince,
"What he would have wanted". And for us
who used the bench, the shower, the floor
where the evening before we'd found him.

After work he'd run the length of the beach,
jogging past the poor families, the giggling
couples, the day-trippers, cutting
through the funfair — *Twenty-first Century Wheel,
House of Mirrors, the Log Flume*
and back to the out-of-season squash club,
that empty, echoing room.

We took it in turns with the young copper
and the ambulance men. We'd pummelled and blown
into his cold chest until
doing that became a silent shouting
into the cave, and so we came out
into the evening sunshine and the hot-dog smells
and the screams of the gulls and then
said *Fuck* and held each other
and cried like men.

Angel on the Line

One rainy afternoon, on time,
the usual stretch between Swansea and Neath,
an angel flies into his windscreen
and he slams the brakes. Beneath

his straightforward weight of wheels
she goes. He feels the impact as in a dream.
Her life flashes and is splintered by steel
as the metals spark her unheard scream.

The passengers tidy their strewn papers
and bags. They are hushed
by the guard's awkward news. Someone coughs,
there's a low crying, and then proper

silence. They move off again, the train
on tiptoe. Some whisper, others just stare
at the glass of the smeared afternoon
and the faces shown to the faces there.

The blunt, blind engine pulls them away
from whatever mess the growing rain
washes from the track. So they
go home, each to a changed destination.

A Sloping House

Megan showed me into the front room
where he'd watched away his nights
and weekends with sport and game shows.
He lay, I supposed, professionally posed
in a shut coffin that filled the room.
I remembered the Tenby lifeboat we used to visit
in its sloping house, ready to slip away,
or one of the locos he drove
at night, locked and cooled in its place
in the Carmarthen sheds.

"Jim suffered so much. Shrunk to a shadow
of himself," she said, and turned
(I thought for a hankie, but instead)
for a freshener spray can to send
instant mist wreathing with dew
the box and its flowers arranged on the lid.
"Passed top of his driver's course in England," she said.
"He propped that season for Moseley," I said,
"and taught me all the front-row tricks."
The chemical bouquet filled my nose like smoke.

At Morriston we saw him off, shunted
down the line with all the others that day.
Like his brother, my dad, it was *The Old Rugged Cross*.
The Organist trod the pedals in her stockinged feet,
but played, at least, like it meant something.
Three things stay with me — those nyloned toes dancing;
the sweet, false flower smell when Megan anointed
herself and me and Jim between; and her hands

kneading a bunched white handkerchief
until it was a hard stone to be rolled away.

Haiku

A tree falls, someone
you love dies — the same hurt space,
same shudder of light.

Rope Tricks

Down the sheer, windowed wall
of the university hospital wing
two figures absail for charity.

It is a fine June evening, soft shadows
playing against the brick and glass
making it rock and ice.

An audience of friends and staff
cheers as each in turn spiders down.
Half-way, one risks a bravura wave.

Their progress is by halting, jerky moves,
a sponsored, visible taking of risks,
the absurd harness, the slippage of rope.

Applause and shouts float up to the surgical wards
like a distant game, something from another time
somewhere, recorded and played back.

From those curtained, drip-feed beds
it seems like another escape attempt, prisoners
out in the world and hanging by a thread.

Aubade

Through the morning traffic's din
a trickle of water from the throat of a robin
that bobs and twitches in the stalks of the elder
the parliament of birds have stripped all summer.
Each year I say: such waste, we should use them
— elderberry wine or elder-flower champagne,
but there's never the time. So birds feed,
shit blue that smears under our wipers, bleed
a sky wash of the passing, generous fruit
that colours our way to the city.
But now this robin's watery throat
halts my turn of the ignition key,
makes me walk back to the garden seat
for a late summer song that fills, then leaves me.

Coracle

Sea Oracle—
wattled water rider, sewin slayer,
Towy tossed when the tide rises.
Man-shell — two tortoises
crawling from the falling sun,
or the wings of a black moth.
Two halves of a cockleshell
drifting back to a whole.

One arm twisting like ivy
round the smooth paddle
to stir the water like thick cawl,
the other weighing the net's haul
from its slow semi-circle of river-trawl.
And then the unstrapped truncheon,
brought down for the sharp crack of bone,
the last slap of dispatch.

Thimbles worn against
the current's sharpening point
with their slung-between fish-pen,
gill-snagging, fin-trapping,
cow hair spun into strings
that play the deep song of the river.
The catch of silver
in the midas touch of moonlight.

Reg Webb

had sailed the five oceans
putting out from Cardiff, Singapore, Boston,
he'd cork-screwed merchantmen
through icy shoals of Atlantic U-boats, then
in peace, piloted the fat oil hulks through
the maze of the Haven's rocky green and blue,
with their confusion of pipes to nuzzle
and suckle the Milford terminals.

Reg, landlocked for years in an armchair
in front of the tv's babble, stared
at his chipboard fire-place, the china,
chintz and brass, the gaudy gilt mirror.
Awash with bile, incontinent, bilges leaking,
his eyes watery and vast, was past pottering
with the roses and bulbs of the flat's
flower border, and shooing away cats.

Reg, becalmed in the straits of morphine
captaining his bed, full-sheeted, trim,
away from the port of his front room and tv,
the photo at the Palace for his O.B.E.
floundering and sick of being ill,
sank angrily, far out in the cottage hospital.
He's lost now, with fire in the hold, and a hard stoke
for one last evasive action, making smoke.

Walking on Water

God ud a given us web feet
if he'd meant us...

But William Llewellyn walked away from Tenby
on the sea.
From the Royal Victoria Pier
towards St Catherine's Rock he walked

while the gawping crowd cheered
then threw their hats as he returned slowly,
safely back to their assembled witness
and a third of the pier receipts that day.

Oh, this was better than Mrs Pankhurst,
better than Jan Kubelik who fiddled like a humming bird,
better than Chevalier or John McCormack — this was a first —
better than Hackenschmidt, wrestling champion of the world!

Each year after, until 1907, he walked the sea,
along the South Beach, across Lydstep Haven,
his cockleshell boats clumsy
as grown-up shoes on a toddler.

And then the London Animatograph Company
made a motion picture film for Llewellyn
to walk through the music halls of England
from John O'Groats to Land's End.

The gas-lights dim, the machine clanks and whirrs,
throwing grey flickering dreams through the thick air.
A man in giant boots slide-shuffles through waves
— he is puppet and puppeteer,

a man discovering quicksand, or that farm boy
full of ale who finds himself wading
in grass he remembers cutting that day
and not believing his legs.

Under an October sun still warm,
sweating in his oilskin trousers
he steers the chariot of himself
towards an impossible horizon.

Half-way to exhaustion he stops,
laboriously, miraculously
he turns and, arms raised wide for balance,
nails his cross to the sea.

The New Settlement

It were planting time when I went
to hear them in Pembroke hall. The All British Settlement —
loads of work for everyone, free land,
an hundred acres a man, if you was fit, they said.
I thought, well, Mary has made me a fool, I'm fit,
fit to go from Jeffreyston to a new life. And kept
"under the Old Flag", as they put it.
Not that I was alone. They must have signed a hundred.

For all the sun here it is still green with trees
so great they do make an English oak a thistle,
with rivers that make the Cleddau a stream
and skies big as the ocean we crossed.
The sound of the train carries over with a north breeze.
And if it is evening I hear a whistle from that metal line
stretching across to Ontario and ships and more rails
all laid into a road home to the old country.

Here it is sheep and corn, not potatoes,
but in the Settlement, earth is still earth
as sure as was in Carew, Cresselly, or Cold Blow.
Why Mary should have done that to me, I don't know.
Us courting hard, close to being engaged, and him
a known philanderer — her skirt up round her waist when
I opened the barn door. This black letter sent a month ago
calls me back, so I'll go — train, sea and all. Single berth.

The old man rolling drunk from Narberth market
in the pitch of night turned the cart over
and snapped his neck like a turkey's, so they write.
I want none of the old farm. Best to sell up, return
to this land. Slip quiet into the village and out
with the solicitor man doing the palaver.
Weeks to get there and back again. Skies do narrow and widen
as we move about — Saskatchewan, Jefferyston, Saskatchewan.

Sutherland at Picton Ferry

At his back
the salt-sour murmur of the tide,
the rustle and crackle of reeds
at that moment they change
supple green to starched yellow.

At his back the woods and garden's purples and pinks,
azaleas, rhododendrons,
clutches of brief colour in the early summer sun.
In Wales they grow in masses on the old-money estates
like weeds for the crach-ach.

The curl-ee, curl-ee, curl-ee,
then the bird climbs into the air
to skim over the river, a single letter
written against the far bank, down the eastern Cleddau
into a freshening breeze off the sea that moves
the reeds, the leaves, the water and clouds
at his back, unseen but necessary
to the roots he stares at so the looking,
because of the otherness of all these things,
changes what is looked at,
and the roots define the hollows and shades
brown earth has caught
in the convolutions of space in the form.
And then there is no river, no sky
no curlew's cry, no reeds, no Pembrokeshire,
but shapes and space only.

He peers at the form, in below the great bole
of the tree rampant above him as a leopard's head
— blunt with eyes and the line of a mouth —
and the roots are sinews of a neck,
the muscles and ligaments of a strength
held in the bank, displayed
by the tide's scalpel.

He looks and looks until
the earth, the tree, the salt smell of the estuary
fold into pure form and become
torso, cave, grave, cruciform.

Two Augustus John Poems

Caitlin Macnamara

He sees a gypsy princess, seventeen,
head proudly high and turned to the future
— that would be Dylan and children,
the loving fights at Laugharne and the ocean flight
to her marble cherub slabbed in Manhattan.

But here it is still rose-bloom, tumbling hair,
neck like a waterfall crashing in the light
to firm breasts Augustus John
eyed until it hurt, neglecting the detail
of hands on hips, the folds of her skirt.

She flames with a young woman's fire
and he, mid-life, the blaze of his beard
and hair dimming, would lead her
to Dylan, paint *the happy schoolboy* and later
punch him flat with jealousy on the Carmarthen road.

He sees her glow and swell with her womanhood
set there on a reclaimed canvas so that hidden
in her womb she has the inverted head
of an abandoned sitter, a dark-haired woman
who stares. A ghost patterned in the pullover

that he would rise to adjust,
and in adjusting open, remove
and let fall to the studio floor.
What is it this painting loves?
Youth, breasts, hair — the persistent ghost?

And did she, seeing it finished,
feel the user or the used?
Whatever feelings the paint fixed that day
are held half a life, half a legend away.
Museum piece, catalogue note, truth and art confused.

Inspiration

The brain is bathed in blood — Dannie Abse

Was it Dorelia's breasts under a loose blouse?
Ida's ninth-month child-cavern of a stomach?
Caitlin's cataract of hair?

The princess's *Indian Herb* offered in the salon?
The sweet reek of a gypsy fire
under a fresh, split rabbit?

The smoky music light of Montmartre?
The dip and rise of the ballroom
as the famous danced over the ocean?

Or this —

a dive off Giltar Point into cool sea
that plunged him through seaweed
to butt the hidden rock.

Staggering back with the flap
of his scalp held in one bloody hand,
laughing out loud,

the sting of salt
throwing his head back to the red sky
and the jeering gulls,

his feet pressed firmly
into the mortal sway
of the wet sand.

The Captain's Diary

1909. On the whole, a good year. By chance
the summer has left the grass full and strong
after our uncommonly late winter.
The new half of nine holes is settling down,
though the greens will, no doubt, need years longer.
Rabbits continue to create a damn nuisance;
the professional has borrowed a shotgun.

We have resolved at last, with common sense,
the issue of the women. Surely it is bad
enough encountering them on the course without ceding
government of the Tenby club to them. The ladies,
some of them, may play decently enough, but having
their own captain and secretary gives them
all the say they need without hampering
the business of the club with their chatter and whinge.
Now they have Miss Adela Voyle, if you please,
as their "Captain" and the trappings of their own club.
All this won without platform, chains or a food syringe!

A greater number of visitors this summer.
Caught one fellow using a cleek — a cleek!
— off the seventh tee. *Use your driver, sir!*
A driver, if you please. I sent him packing
and will keep an eye out for him in future.
These visitors contribute to the revenue lacking
but nothing justifies such impertinent cheek.

High tides will prove a problem should we persist
with those holes along the South Beach
for that fine prospect of Caldey Island and the coast.
The Rev. Morris proclaims that if God had
meant there to be a golf course here then He
would have marked one out. Sometimes Morris has a manner
too flip for the propriety of his calling.
(I answered him with a belch.)
We were at the sherry decanter, be it said.
Though our most celebrated guest seemed to welcome
that sort of banter. His Majesty's Chancellor
proved to be a passable hitter of the ball,
though prone to take in the view too much
to consider seriously the challenge of the golfing.
It is said that he will cut a road
in the history of our empire. Certainly,
it is held to be a matter of note for the Welsh
that one of their number be counted in such office.

He is of no great height for a man of coming greatness
and his eyes dart at times like a goat's,
not wishing to miss one moment. Except on a tee,
I am here thinking of the Black Rock from which, as I say,
his gaze was something of a dreamer's.
This land, he said, (and all the time,
to my intense irritation, he called me "Doctor M")
it is as if a giant had scooped the grass and sand.
Or great engines of war had gouged the earth in bites,
that now grows back to heal its wounds.
Which I thought smacked too fully of the poet
and too little of the real man.
Though, in truth, there were rifle cracklings aplenty
as we passed the Lifter's Cottage, playing the Railway
and holes through to the Penally Butts.

It is my belief that we have recovered completely,
as a body of sportsmen, if not in our fiscal health,
from the loss of that land to the Army.
What seemed indeed a hard blow four years ago when all
our efforts to build an 18-hole course were washed away
as surely as if the sea rose over us in storm,
we have now had to put behind us. The Army's needs etcetera...
Though Mr Lloyd George seemed not inclined to deal
with this German Navy business when the vicar,
that fool Morris, raised it at dinner.
For my part, I think the Powers shall resolve matters
as good managers ought with the world's affairs.
God preserve us from another engagement. The Boers...
These riflemen on the ranges at Penally are like golfers
at their practice. In readiness for the game.

The Tradesmen's Club issue has now been resolved.
I for one see little harm, provided their play
is restricted. They will prove useful in maintenance work.
However, the trial of the early closing day
free golf for the shop class could open up doors
best left closed. A course supervised by James Braid,
Champion of the British Isles, must needs be strictly governed.
It was my honour to partner Braid in a medal fours.

Morris has word that Mathias-Thomas has bought the four holes
belonging to Davies's land. I think this bodes ill,
for while Lord Davies of Llandinam has much
to occupy himself with his empire of coals,
(not to mention Lloyd George's tilt at the Upper House)
Mathias-Thomas will surely look to catch a profit
from his acquisition. At the least, my land —
the marshes up to Black Pool — is secure yet,
and could, if needed, bring some three further

holes into play. This land business,
and the continuing pressure for Sunday golf
darkens further the prospect of the impending winter.
Already the mornings are chill and the wind
from the Irish Sea cuts through tweed like a bayonet.

Playing St. Enodoc's

i.m. John Betjeman

From the First the bay of Daymer
glistened in its summer blue
and the clouds from the Atlantic
formed a high, white, patient queue.

No rain threatened, sun was warming
Saint Enodoc's bent spire
leaning seawards like a stone sail
set by a sailors' ghostly choir.

Cleared the Sixth's sand Himalayas
after scuffing one away,
took a five and felt elated
where a five's good any day.

Hit a big one down the Thirteenth,
from the fairway used a four
to the green above the Churchyard —
missed my birdie, missed my par —

where Sir John, his scrolled slate headstone
standing in the springy turf,
rests in peace and metred decay
in death's awful breach of love,

just a niblick from the flag-stick
where he holed once. For all time
triumph savoured in the nostrils
with the blossom and the brine.

Walking down the Eighteenth fairway
back towards the town of Rock
and the harbour's nodding sailboats
having played St. Enodoc's

for the sport, and too, in homage
to a man of golf and rhyme
who, once, birdied at the Thirteenth.
Oh, how splendid. Quite sublime!

The Poetry of Money

*There's no money in poetry, but then
there's no poetry in money.*
— Robert Frost

The shilling takes a king's head.

The marque of the Mark;
The frog marched Franc.

The nous of the Yen;
The cold, cold Krona.

Credit transfer.

Dirt packed under the fingernails
for crisp lettuce in the fist.

The shackles of the Shekels.
Running the marathon of the mortgage.

The tyranny of the Talents.

The swelling goytre of debt:
The brief bouquet of the winnings.

The sun-glinting curl of the incoming loan
before the shale-pull of the debit.

The distant ochre hills of the Drachma.

The Punt, an indistinguishable craft,
floats down our river.

The Ecu perches in its cave of guano
and preens itself.

The Lira buys Rome.

The underwriter grips the rail
and curses the storm.

What's worse — the plastic in the lock,
or the lock in the plastic?

The rustle of old invoices.

Have no truck with their shop —
bite into the coin you have.

The chime of a dime,
a death in the quarter

and the buck never stops.

Slight as a wren, the farthing
sings to the widow.

Still a bankroll thick enough
to choke a horse.

The dull brass rub of a Crown.

Five Poems from the Dialect
of the Iraqi Marsh Arabs
By Mudhafer Al Nawab

Translated by

Tony Curtis
&
Mustafa Hadi

Mudhafer Al Nawab —

is an Iraqi poet, born in 1932, from a distinguished Baghdad family. He started writing poems in a southern colloquial Iraqi when he was a young man. He is regarded by many as the founder of the colloquial Iraqi romantic school of poetry. He left Iraq in the 1970s because of his political activities. He has become more involved in the Palestinian struggle in recent years. He now writes in orthodox Arabic.

To the Train and Hammad

On the morning water she fell in love with him...
on the night water there was a moon and a train passed by.

On the night train
We passed by you, Hammad
And heard the sound of coffee grinding
And cardamom scent filled the air.
O train cry, O train
Sigh gently as you go by,
Beneath the swaying corn the grouse lie.

You are more beautiful than I —
You wear a turquoise ring in your nose,
Your bracelets jangle as you run from me —
O train, as you go by Umm Shammat,
Go temptingly, in the night,
Don't make the goodbye run —
My heart hasn't yet died.
Sigh gently as you go by,
Beneath the corn the grouse still lie.

O empty wagons, rumble by,
Pass this station with sorrow and wail.
We didn't enjoy our love for long —
How could I have hoped for more?
O train, breathe sorrow in your steam
Over the lovers laden with pain.
Sigh gently as you go by.
Beneath the stirring corn grouse lie.

O train, if those cries were false,
Then would our love be unreal?
If all my life were travelled with you
The fire would not be quenched,

Not even if your straight tracks became mine.
Sigh gently as you go by —
Beneath the corn grouse lie.

I want to live for Hammad
Of Umm Shammat,
And no-one but him.
The sunshine and the morning breeze
Startle me as I awake remembering
How we played together — our hide-and-seek,
Piggyback right into our early teens,
Before convention wrenched us apart.
Now, as then,
Sigh gently as you go by,
Beneath the corn the grouse lie.

Hammad is dowry silver,
He's a smoking pipe
Tattooed with turquoise water
When I see his shirt tucked up from the waist.
Slow down, O train and let me whisper
To him. Maybe the sorrow in my whisper
Will make the grouse yearn.

Like a handful of warmth
The morning breeze gathers my breasts
Till the empty wagons make me shiver.
O train, don't spook me again,
You'll only excite the pain.
Let the hurt slip away with the breeze I sigh —
Beneath my blouse these grouse lie.

Your hair fringes the sun and air
Together. They are a wedding cry,
Or skeins of harvested clovers
Trickling gold through my lover's comb.
Your patience is as long as hair,
Train, you can go on by,
See how the breeze you stir
Lulls the grouse to sleep.

Just as eyes may be filled
With songs and stories,
Breasts overflow with love,
Our love has risen, then drifted away
Like a boat with no oars,
Leaving Umm Shammat.
Train, sigh gently as you go by —
Beneath the ripe corn the grouse lie.

Knocked Flat

I was knocked out — that breast
with but the weight of a mole!
Whoever bends to kiss there
drowns with the aroma
of rose water.
Who ever made that waist
to fit a bracelet...
knocked me flat!

Your brown beauty sings
like a wedding gasp
or springs of pure raisin juice.
I bathed in sweet sultanas...
you pleasured my heart beyond cure.
That breast weakened mine...
knocked me out!

You hide in your naiveté
and the warmth of Anber rice you offer.
Add more cardamom and serve me
the finest, sobering shummar coffee.
Your curved, full frock stabs me
like a dagger.
I'm knocked out!

The smell of you is blossom
dew-fallen. I'm incensed with it!
My rich-born girl raised with such gifts —
why has prosperity such a slim waist,
sharp enough to cut diamonds
that would madden the richest man?
Knocked flat... I'm knocked out!

A Liar

I wanted you...though you are a liar.
I wanted you even as you sprinkled
my life with handfuls of pain.
I wanted you like breath at an open window,
though my lungs fill with street-dust.
A blush shades my face
from gossip. But you are a liar,
you fox, lurking below sweet grapes
that love you,
love you even as a liar.

You knocked my door —
which splintered with blind joy,
the wood smouldering.
My cheek flamed, my soul burned,
earrings melted in the acid of your gaze.
I neighed, swung my plaits...
my love...my love...my love...
and died over and over again.
They said my heart gave you up,
was cured of you. But, liar,
you stole the bunched grapes of it —
my heart... you fox.
Born liar.

Twice Robbed

In your belt are the keys
to all stories...
and, you know, we lost
the door and the key.

Your nightdress is like a sail:
it tells the fishes the story
of blossom; it tells
the waves the myth of horizons.

Tell those stories again,
before another parting
beckons, steals you,
my love, from us.

Yesterday they took you away.
They asked me to describe you.
What does he do?
What is he like?

I was confused,
so that not even I knew.
Their questioning
perplexed me.

I grew weary of it —
I showed them my heart
and said,
Does any of the keys fit?

The Summer-rain is Coming

...and then the night came... and the wind after...

Be green my heart, green, I beg you.
This is our last affair.
Be green and give all you can of roses
now the summer-rain has come,
pulling invisible flowers into the air,
colouring the dry world.
Give all you have to the gentle breeze
before the rough winds shake us,
my love, my very soul.

The next lover knocks my door,
and I'll go to him, I know,
give myself. He'll wear
me like a cuff-link!

I bet tonight even the barren heath
will have some rain,
even the bare branch
will have leafed the beginnings
of new branches,
and I'm still waiting.

I see it —
before the year has passed,
there'll be green everywhere,
growing over the steps to my door
twining around the door-lock
springing it open.

Oh, my heart — how long you'll sorrow,
I said to myself —

maybe you're empty of meaning,
barren. I said,
maybe it's thirst of love
that makes you so bare — not even a mushroom
growing, nothing — and yet
I dream of roses!

My heart,
traitor I have grown,
now the summer-rain comes
I forgive you.

The Pew

The Llancarfan Baptists pew we've used
in our front bedroom's bay
is clothes-horse, book shelf, bric-a-brac display.
My jeans agape, your shoulder bags, bra,
all strapped things hooked over one end.
These pieces of our life are
icons of our lapsing century's close.
Such use would offend that stiff
arrangement of posed deacons John Thomas froze
in 1887 when he unlidded his lens.
Their goodness and sin each dark Sunday
congealed in the stark chapel's gloom.
What was their vision of glory and doom?
We'll read about such beliefs,
not feel their weight. We act only on
the present, what's quick and revealed here.
Outside the morning grows traffic fumes and din.
The sudden sun picks out the skeleton of air,
motes of house dust and our skin.

More and more

More and more I cry now
afterwards, each time
it seems I cry.
And he never asks why.
He stares beyond me
over my left shoulder
into the pillow.
He himself feels heavy,
he says,
and his voice thickens,
his nose, still dry,
fills with feeling.
He remembers sea water
after the first plunge.
His heart's piston driving
as it did when he ran for
a ball's mazy bobble
grubber-kicked over the line.
A race to touch down
he was always going to lose
and did.

The Eagle

rang through the air to my glove
fisted around the dead chick

they'd primed it with. At the last moment
I closed my eyes and turned my head,

always fearful of feathers and claws.
But knew the bird from its distanced weight,

both landing and flight held balanced on the arm,
its pliant grip and perch on me

that was an otherness, like
no other feeling in the world

except, perhaps, a slow, wonderful fuck
and the dream of being in love.

Soap Opera

We are woken in the early hours,
our hands clearing lines of sight
through condensation on the windows.

Pulled from sleep's long downward reach
into what we dream and wish, we watch
the soap opera of a warring couple in the street —

...a drink or two... having dinner...
thought you... never wanted... fuck off home...
you come back here...

They circle in the sour pool of the street light,
and we are curtained witnesses to a moment's ugliness
all four of us will, at different speeds, forget.

Back under the duvet we brush lips goodnight
then move apart to each one's side of the bed
where dreams collide with the words unsaid.

Out on the road, beyond our gates
and high privet hedge, the taxis throttle
away out of town to the estates.

Now you shiver and curl right to the edge
— for my hand was chilled by the damp pane it wiped
to show night, sad voices, a web of uncertain light.

Coeurs de Plomb

To your definitions of love
add this —
the cold, young, still-white
breast lifted
and from the rib-cage,
by a skilled and gentle knife,
the heart released.

Bloody pump, valves and all,
device, design, tired metaphor,
that which is given and taken,
lost and won.
Now claimed in love
embalmed and cased in lead
perpetual.

And to your definitions of death
add this —
that love should ache so much
to cut and seal
the shadow of itself
to cheat the idea of death
with a closed, lead heart.

Queen's Tears

In ten years, not once have these colours shown.
Inherited with our house
then relegated to my college room,
its dull green-margined petals
have filled my window space for two years.
And now *Billbergia Windii*, Queen's Tears
sends five tendrils out with five pink sepals,
each unclenching a pendant of flowers,
blue and yellow and red.

I inherited the room, too. David
tall and balding, fiftyish, worked here —
incongruous suit and acting pumps,
an English voice that could be powerful or plum.
It's four years since he died. A Fulbright
to California did for him —
long afternoons cruising for lovers in the sun,
anonymous bath-house couplings at night.

He sat in the office as they phoned the doctor.
I saw him there, shaking with the sweats,
his slack mouth caked with saliva.
His mind had gone beyond us. Staring ahead
he knew what was plain for us to see.

He had no family. At the funeral, actress
friends from his drama school days
did something from Proust, a Donne sonnet
beautifully read, to an audience
of colleagues and dutiful boss.

Another spring is due, the magnolia tree
knocks against the window. My first floor
view frames an angle of buildings
and the sky's parade of clouds behind
the failing *Queen's Tears*.

David, let the deep green, loud red
and ice blue sing for you
and all the casual folk I never really knew,
but think of on occasions, remotely, from the past,
as now. Brief flowerings that come
unannounced, and do not last.

Summer in Bangkok

The second day he bought a wife
for his stay.
He kept her in his room and fucked
her all the ways he'd ever dreamed.
She was fed and kept
and smiled and answered his needs.

It was perfect, save that her English
was a dozen, broken sentences.

Some days he would go to see the city:
then she ran herself clean under the shower,
she moved around the room trailing her hand
over polished wood, curtains, picture frames.
She lay on the bed he tied her to.

And in the final week he took the interior trek
— eight guys led into the hills
and poisonous snakes, bare-teeth monkeys.
They burned leeches from their arms and legs.
In the trees were men with guns and heroin eyes.
Their women were invisible, their children sold to the city

Each night he shivered. They were locked
in by the massive dark, a wall of sounds.
Like children they went to piss in pairs.
When he looked up the sky was small. He saw
no plough, no bear, no hunter.
The stars would not be read.

On the fourth day they struck the river and turned,
made bamboo rafts with poles and rode the white water
back to the coast, the skyscrapers, the wild taxis,
the silk, the child beggars, career amputees.

Halfway, they poled a long, slow curve and met
the heroin men on both banks, rifles raised
and aimed at them. Their guide spoke loudly
and quickly, his hands eloquent, then fevered,
the rest kept still on the bobbing water.
He gripped his pole tightly, all he could do,
so it stuck and trembled in the river bottom.
He had no words.

Back on the hotel she lay on his bed,
her hair spread wet on his pillow, her arms
and legs, as it were, swimming.

In Union Square, 1978

The pigeons perch and shit on Dewy's column
for the Manila Bay defeat of the Spanish,
Each side of the plinth someone
has outlined the deathshape of a man
with bloodstains like spilt sodapop or paint or gum.
The form is chalked as for a victim,
though I know I sleep face down like that.

From the galleries back along Powell
for nine thousand bucks
you can buy a Chagall —
A boy who flies, a violin,
limited edition.

This is San Francisco
crossed by the chocolate and cream cable-cars
that climb and fall the bumps
and bell the long day through,
where a quarter takes from Downtown
to the Bridge and a jump
across the bay to Alcatraz.

A breeze moves the warm air
and the little *chicano* girl's hand slips
the string. In Union Square
her silver donut balloons rise
against the big neon palms,
Frank Sinatra playing Reno
and the Lake Tahoe girls with feathered tits,
up and beyond the glass elevators
as they crawl the outside of the St. Francis,
above the office lunchers on the lawn,
the chalk man, over Polk Street

where records and books are open and gay
away above Chinatown and the wax museum,
Fisherman's Wharf on the green bay
and the city warming itself in the easy sun.

Brady's Glass

The senator's wife herself served us — tossed
fresh salad with the finest ham:
full cured Virginia, at god knows what cost,
the tomatoes somewhat underripe, but fat.

Our conversation turned to the war
— Lee's retreat and his scorching of the South —
until a crash of glass brought Silus
and the other boy to the door.

His barrow had tipped against the glasshouse, splinters
were scattered like ice all around. "Brady's glass,"
the Senator said, "his photographist's pictures
from Antietam, when we held against Jackson.

The dead at Sharpsburg, at the Bloody Lane —
most distressing. The public's sense of shock
was very regrettable. The plates he left
were just the size for hot house panes."

Silus fitted fresh glass from a stock
he kept in the stables. Faint grey ghosts fallen
in a dirt road ditch with awkward limbs
and bloated bellies, backs arched in pain.

All that summer the sun shone through
those stiffened dead, printing them
on to the green leaves and ripening crop,
bruises in the fruit that were grey and blue.

From the hills, the town

As he talks he rolls an apple in his hands
which with the force of his thumbs
he splits to make two glistening
full-waxed moons of sweet flesh.
Below, the town is a mouth of broken teeth.
In his mind it is geometry, lines form a grid
— the runway, the mosques, the bread shops.
His face is a map of the long year.

Stones and mortars. But now it is a quiet time.
Though the day still has warmth, his men huddle
around a stove, the smoke of bacon, coffee.
Suddenly hungry, his eyes blink wide.
He fits the two apple halves back together
and bites from one, then the other.

Belgium: Coffee

Over the Channel England and France
are held in the same small cabin window
and what parts us seems barely chance,
a length of ship-creased water.

Coffee is served over France and Belgium
with the villages and ploughed fields
laid out neatly between the clouds
that catch and buffet the plane.

Here where it is flat and rich we turned
before the Blitzkrieg and fell back in disorder,
in ill-fitting uniforms, rifles kept from Ypres.
Horses were drowned, trucks ditched and burned.

The ragged flotilla — weekend fishing boats
pleasure-trippers, anything that would float,
ferried home those dregs of an army
that in time became mythologically cheery.

These clouds held dog-fights
on such summer days as this — the height
we have gives us a grand view
down over the blue air they smoked through.

As we descend, bumping through cumulus,
he illuminates the Fasten Seat Belt sign,
the drinks trolley clatters and coffee, mine,
spills hot and sticky on my leg.

Incident on a hospital train
from Calcutta, 1944

At a water-stop three hours out
the dry wail of brakes ground us down
from constant jolting pain to an oven
heat that filled with moans and shouts
from wards the length of six carriages.

We had pulled slowly up towards the summer
hills for coolness. They were hours distant,
hazy and vague. I opened the grimy
window to a rush of heat
and, wrapped in sacking, a baby

held up like some cooked offering from its mother —
Memsahib...meri buchee ko bachalo...Memsahib take —
pushed like an unlooked-for gift into my arms.
She turned into the smoke and steam.
I never saw her face.

As we lumbered off I unwrapped
a dirty, days-old girl, too weak for cries.
Her bird weight and fever-filled eyes
already put her out of our reach. By Murree Junction
that child would have emptied half our beds.

At the next water-stop my nurses left her.
The corporal whose arms had gone looked up at me
and said, *There was nothing else to do.*
Gangrenous, he died at Murree a week later.
His eyes, I remember, were clear, deep and blue.

The Night-trees

Again in the ninth month
he takes his spade to the field.

This is in the late evening
when the darkness is down
and his neighbours indoors.

Slowly he digs a hole —
a tree for a boy: for a girl, a grave.
And this is the fifth time.

He sits there on the broken ground
until the village lights go out
and the fires die. Until
the sun shapes the morning hills.

She has worked all evening at a blanket,
resting it on her stomach.
All night she lies listening.
The hole is out of hearing.

Then each night until her time
she wakes early and in the heavy dark
listens for wind, the rustle of leaves
from his three trees

or the night-birds flying
to perch there with the soft sounds
girls might whisper
one to the other.

Portrait of the Painter Hans Theo Richter and his wife Gisela in Dresden, 1933

This is the perfect moment of love —
Her arm around his neck,
Holding a rose.

Her wisps of yellow hair
The light turns gold.
Her face is the moon to his earth.

Otto's studio wall glows
With the warm wheat glow
Of the loving couple.

This is after the dark etchings,
The blown faces. This is after Bapaume —
The sickly greens, the fallen browns.

She is a tree, her neck a swan's curved to him.
His hands enclose her left hand
Like folded wings.

This is before the fire-storm,
Before the black wind,
The city turned to broken teeth.

It is she who holds the rose to him,
Theo's eyes which lower in contentment
To the surgeon's smock he wears for painting.

This is the perfect moment,
The painted moment
She will not survive.

This is before the hair that flames,
The face that chars. This is before
Her long arms blacken like winter boughs.

This is the harvest of their love,
It is summer in the soul,
The moment they have made together.

From Otto's window the sounds of the day —
The baker's boy calling, a neighbour's wireless
playing marches and then a speech.

The Visit to Terezin

Here are the houses.
There is a light there, and listen
— someone sings.
How clean the streets, yes?
A tidy people, we have observed,
with their own pride.

Here is their bakery and, do you see,
a cobbler, carpenter, the butcher
with their own beliefs
in the killing for meat.
We come to the school. Later we will
be entertained by their orchestra.
A race is redeemed by music, I think.

Look at the children's pictures. You see —
houses with fences. The chimneys smoke
— there are families inside.
A giant — look at his club, his boots.
Where there are children, there will be giants.
And always butterflies, look, so many colours,
they use all the colours,
as large as kites, as large as clouds.
Where a child's mind flies, yes?
This one has played the gallows game.
Or it could be a door.

The bowl and the spoon

Behind the high wire
In a hut under the stilted towers
two women face each other.
Between them a wooden bowl and a spoon.

Each in turn takes the spoon
They hold the bowl with care,
like a rare porcelain, firm,
concentrating the eyes, the fingers.

A spoonful, a spoonful,
another dry swallow
so that still the bowl
holds its same level of soup.

After a while and without words
the daughter at her turn lifts
a spoonful away from her dry mouth
and puts it to her mother's.

She takes the soup, then with her turn
feeds her daughter. In this way
the bowl is tilted and emptied,
only in this way is the spoon licked dry.

A full moon has risen through the wire
like a cut cheese. Light
cat-licks the bowl and spoon
on the bare table.

In this world this is the love we make —
to the strongest the food,
the life to come. Our only grail
an empty spoon.

Acknowledgements

Some of these poems appeared in:
The Poetry Books Society Anthology 2 edited by Anne Stevenson,
Hutchinson, **The Bright Field,** edited by Meic Stephens, Carcanet, **Love
from Wales,** edited by Curtis and James, Seren Books, **High on the
Walls: A Morden Tower Anthology** edited by Brown, Bloodaxe Books,
The Forward Book of Poetry, 1992, *The Barry & District News, The
Cambridge Review, Fine Madness, The Mississippi Valley Review, New
Spokes, The New Welsh Review, Planet, Poetry Digest, Poetry Review, Poetry
Wales, Rialto, Social Care Education, Tar River Poetry, The Tenby Observer,
Quartz, Sources* (translated into French by Christine Pagnoulle).

'Pembrokeshire Buzzards' was a Turret Bookshop Broadsheet.
'Summer in Bangkok' won the 1990 Greenwich Festival Prize.
'Incident on a Hospital Train to Calcutta, 1944' and 'Queen's Tears'
were the poems which won the Dylan Thomas Prize for 1993.

Thanks to Mustafa Hadi who originated the project to produce our
translations of the Mudhafer al Nawab poems.

I must give thanks to the University of Glamorgan and the British
Council for travel grants.

About the Author

Tony Curtis was born in Carmarthen, educated the University College Swansea and Goddard College Vermont. A Senior Lecturer in Creative Writing, he directs the M.A. in Writing at the University of Glamorgan. He is the editor of a number of anthologies and critical works, and the recipient of numerous prizes for his poetry, among them: the Eric Gregory Award and first prize in the National Poetry Competition. He lives with his family in south Wales.